Ultimate Sticker Book
GARDEN BUGS

DK | Penguin Random House

With thanks to Ben Hoare for first edition text
on pages 4–5, 10–11, and 14–15

Project Editor Kritika Gupta
Senior Editor Dawn Sirett
US Senior Editor Shannon Beatty
Senior Art Editor Roohi Rais
Designer Rachael Hare
Managing Editors Monica Saigal, Penny Smith
Managing Art Editor Ivy Sengupta
DTP Designers Sachin Gupta, Syed Md Farhan
Picture Researcher Vagisha Pushp
Jacket Designer Rachael Hare
Jacket Coordinator Magda Pszuk
Production Editor Becky Fallowfield
Production Controller Leanne Burke
Delhi Creative Head Malavika Talukder
Deputy Art Director Mabel Chan
Publisher Francesca Young
Publishing Director Sarah Larter

Royal Horticultural Society
Consultant Andrew Salisbury; **Editor** Simon Maughan
Publisher Helen Griffin; **Head of Editorial** Tom Howard

This edition published in 2024
Previously published as
Ultimate Sticker Book: Bugs and Slugs (2006)
by DK Publishing
1745 Broadway, 20th Floor, New York, NY 10019
in association with The Royal Horticultural Society

Copyright © 2006, 2024 Dorling Kindersley Limited
DK, a Division of Penguin Random House LLC
24 25 26 27 28 10 9 8 7 6 5 4 3 2 1
002-334537-Feb/2024

A catalog record for this book
is available from the Library of Congress.
ISBN: 978-0-7440-8023-0

DK books are available at special discounts when
purchased in bulk for sales promotions, premiums,
fund-raising, or educational use. For details, contact:
DK Publishing Special Markets, 1745 Broadway,
20th Floor, New York, NY 10019
SpecialSales@dk.com

Printed and bound in China

For the curious
www.dk.com

FSC
MIX
Paper | Supporting
responsible forestry
FSC™ C018179

This book was made with Forest
Stewardship Council™ certified
paper—one small step in DK's
commitment to a sustainable future.
For more information go to
www.dk.com/our-green-pledge

Activities

Here are the five different types of activities
that you will find inside this book. Have fun!

Find it!
Hunt for the correct
stickers that fit
the blank spaces.

Follow!
Follow the trail
and put the correct
stickers on the pages.

Match it!
Match the correct
sticker with each picture
to complete the images.

Guess it!
Try the fun sticker
quiz. All the answers
are in the book!

Fit it!
Find the stickers that
fit the blank spaces and
complete the big picture.

Acknowledgments

The publisher would like to thank the following for their kind permission to reproduce their photographs:
(Key: a=above; b=below/bottom; c=center; f=far; l=left; r=right; t=top)

1 Dreamstime.com: Lee Amery (cra); Gale Verhague (tr); Radub85 (br). **Getty Images / iStock:** E+ / Onfokus (tl). **Shutterstock.com:** Bildagentur Zoonar GmbH (bl). **2–3 Dreamstime.com:** Boulanger Sandrine. **2–16 Dreamstime.com:** Aga7ta (Pattern). **3 Dreamstime.com:** Onepony (cl). **4 Alamy Stock Photo:** Nigel Cattlin (tr). **Dreamstime.com:** Marilyn Gould (cla); Gale Verhague (crb). **5 Alamy Stock Photo:** imageBROKER / Reinhard Hlzl (tr); Geoff Smith (cl). **Dreamstime.com:** Oleksii Kriachko (cr). **Shutterstock.com:** Bildagentur Zoonar GmbH (bl). **6–7 Alamy Stock Photo:** Clarence Holmes Wildlife. **8 Alamy Stock Photo:** Custom Life Science Images (cla). **Dreamstime.com:** Isselee (ca/cra). **9 Alamy Stock Photo:** agefotostock / Don Johnston (c). **10 Alamy Stock Photo:** Frank Hecker (cra). **Dreamstime.com:** Mikhail Gnatkovskiy (tr); Vnlit (cr). **Getty Images:** Moment Open / by MedioTuerto (bl). **11 Alamy Stock Photo:** David Whitaker (bl). **Dreamstime.com:** Henk Wallays (br); Alexander Hasenkampf (tc); EPhotocorp (tl). **12 Shutterstock.com:** Anton Kozyrev (c). **12–13 Shutterstock.com:** Anton Kozyrev. **14 Alamy Stock Photo:** Clare Gainey (tr). **Dreamstime.com:** Pornsawan Baipakdee (tl). **Shutterstock.com:** Ant Cooper (clb). **15 Alamy Stock Photo:** DP Wildlife Invertebrates (cl). **Dreamstime.com:** Daniel Larson (crb); Henri Koskinen (tl); Viniciussouza06 (clb). **Shutterstock.com:** Tushar Chindarkar (tr). **16 123RF.com:** leekris (cb). **Alamy Stock Photo:** Nigel Cattlin (cra); David Whitaker (br); Alf Jacob Nilsen (fcra). **Dreamstime.com:** Alexstar (cr); Henk Wallays (crb); Guantana (tc); Ryan Pike (tr); Oleksii Kriachko (cla). **Getty Images / iStock:** E+ / Onfokus (ca). **Shutterstock.com:** Ant Cooper (bl). **18 Alamy Stock Photo:** Alf Jacob Nilsen (clb). **Dorling Kindersley:** Frank Greenaway / Natural History Museum, London (tl), (fbl/X2). **Dreamstime.com:** Guantana (crb); Radub85 (tr), (br/X2); Boulanger Sandrine (Grass BGx9); Onepony (cb), (cra); Ryan Pike (cl); Cosmin Manci (tc), (bl/X2); Daniel Prudek (cra), (fbr/X2); Wabeno (cb); Pavel Parmenov (cb/Earthworm). **19 Alamy Stock Photo:** Nigel Cattlin (tc); imageBROKER / Reinhard Hlzl (ca); Geoff Smith (tr). **Dreamstime.com:** Gale Verhague (clb, fbr/X2); Marilyn Gould (tl, bl/X2); Oleksii Kriachko (cr), (br/X2). **Shutterstock.com:** Bildagentur Zoonar GmbH (cb), (fbl/X2). **22 Alamy Stock Photo:** Clarence Holmes Wildlife (ca/X6), (fbl/X2); Naturepix (tr), (bl/X2). **Dreamstime.com:** Mitya Chernov (cra), (br/X2); Wirestock (cr), (fbr/X2). **23 Alamy Stock Photo:** Nigel Cattlin (clb/X2), (cl); imageBROKER / Reinhard Hlzl (fclb/X2); Geoff Smith (crb/X2); Custom Life Science Images (tl); Clarence Holmes Wildlife (fcrb/X2); Daniel Dempster Photography (ca, c/Pupa, b/X4). **Dreamstime.com:** Isselee (tc), (cr). **123RF.com:** leekris (cla, fbl/x2). **Getty Images / iStock:** E+ / Onfokus (tr, c, br/x2). **Getty Images:** Stone / Paul Starosta (fcl). **26 Alamy Stock Photo:** Frank Hecker (bl/X2); David Whitaker (cb), (crb/X2). **Dorling Kindersley:** Koen van Klijken (tr). **Dreamstime.com:** Henk Wallays (fbr/X2); Alexander Hasenkampf (clb/X2), (cra); Vnlit (ca), (br/X2); EPhotocorp (tc), (fbl/X2); Daniel Prudek (c), (fcrb/X2). **Getty Images / iStock:** E+ / coopder1 (tl), (fclb/X2). **Getty Images:** Moment Open / by MedioTuerto (cl). **27 Alamy Stock Photo:** Frank Hecker (clb/X2). **Dorling Kindersley:** Koen van Klijken (fbl/X2); Frank Greenaway / Natural History Museum, London (fbr/X2); Gale Verhague (br/X2); EPhotocorp (fclb/X2); Artoorek (fcrb/X2); Guantana (crb/X2); Daniel Prudek (bl/X2). **Shutterstock.com:** Anton Kozyrev (t). **30 Alamy Stock Photo:** Clare Gainey (tc), (bl/X2); DP Wildlife Invertebrates (clb). **Dreamstime.com:** Daniel Larson (cb, fbr/X2); Pornsawan Baipakdee (tl); Henri Koskinen (ca); Viniciussouza06 (cr). **Shutterstock.com:** Ant Cooper (cla), (br/X2); Tushar Chindarkar (cra), (fbl/X2). **31 Alamy Stock Photo:** Nigel Cattlin (clb/X2); imageBROKER / Reinhard Hlzl (fclb/X2); Geoff Smith (crb/X4); Clarence Holmes Wildlife (fcrb/X2); DP Wildlife Invertebrates (fclb/SilverfishX2). **Dreamstime.com:** Daniel Larson (fcrb/beetleX2); Gale Verhague (fbr/x2); Henk Wallays (fclb/beetleX2); Pornsawan Baipakdee (fcrb/CockroachX2); Henri Koskinen (clb/WoodlouseX2); Viniciussouza06 (crb); Oleksii Kriachko (br/beetleX2). **Getty Images / iStock:** E+ / Onfokus (bl/x2). **Shutterstock.com:** Bildagentur Zoonar GmbH (fbl/X2); Tushar Chindarkar (clb/FlyX2).

Cover images: *Front:* **Dorling Kindersley:** Frank Greenaway / Natural History Museum, London cla; **Dreamstime.com:** Marilyn Barbone cbl/ (X2), Alexander Hasenkampf cb, Isselee clb, Daniel Prudek cla/ (hornet), Radub85 tr; **Getty Images / iStock:** Antagain cra, ranasu (X4); *Back:* **Dreamstime.com:** Marilyn Barbone cbl/ (X2); **Getty Images / iStock:** Antagain cra, ranasu (X5)

All other images © Dorling Kindersley

Bugs in the garden

There's a whole world of bugs in a garden. With lots of plants to eat, soil to burrow in, and trees for shelter, gardens provide bugs with everything they might need to survive.

Butterfly

Moth

Beetle

Beetles come in different shapes and sizes. These insects usually have hard wing cases that protect their delicate flying wings. More than one-third of all the insects in the world are beetles.

Butterfly and moth

There are lots of different butterflies and moths. Usually found near flowers, these insects have two pairs of broad wings, which can be covered in beautiful patterns.

Beetle

Centipede

Centipede and millipede

Centipedes and millipedes are usually found on or in soil. They both have many body segments. Millipedes have two pairs of legs per body segment. Centipedes have one pair of legs per body segment.

Millipede

Spider

There are several types of predatory bugs that prey on other bugs in a garden. Spiders are one of these predatory bugs. Spiders are not insects. All insects have six legs, whereas all spiders have eight legs.

Yellow jacket

Spider

Honeybee and yellow jacket

If you look closely, you can see differences between honeybees and yellow jackets. While yellow jackets have long bodies and are bright yellow and black in color, honeybees are rounder and look more orange.

Honeybee

Earthworm

Earthworms have soft, thin bodies. They spend most of their lives underground, tunneling their way through the soil and mixing it up. Their digging helps plants grow.

Earthworm

Plant-eaters

There's an army of small creatures that love to eat the plants in a garden. Different parts of plants are gobbled up, including new green shoots, leaves, and sugary flower nectar.

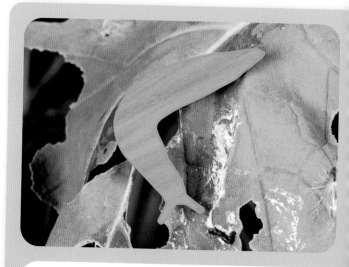

Common garden slug

Slugs are most active at night. This is when they usually feed. The common garden slug munches on leaves, shoots, and thickened underground stems called tubers. It also eats rotting plants and poop.

Monarch butterfly

Butterflies drink nectar. Monarch butterflies visit a variety of flowers for nectar. Monarch caterpillars only eat milkweed plants.

Hummingbird moth

This moth flies in the daytime and hovers to sip nectar from flowers. As it hovers, its wings beat fast, and it looks like a hummingbird. So that's the bird it's named after!

Hoverflies feed on nectar and pollen. They look like wasps, which means other animals don't eat them because wasps sting and taste bad.

Puss moth caterpillar

If threatened, this odd-looking creature flashes the red markings on its face and whips its tail around. The puss moth caterpillar eats the leaves of willow and poplar trees. This caterpillar turns into a moth that's so fluffy it's named after a pussycat!

Bumblebee

Like other bees, the bumblebee drinks nectar. It is big and hairy, and flies more slowly than some other bees, and makes a much louder buzzing noise, too.

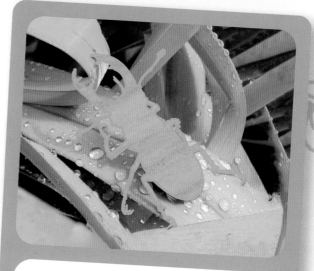

Stag beetle

A stag beetle can be up to 3 in (7.5 cm) long. Young stag beetles (called larvae) feed on rotting wood, such as tree stumps, while adult stag beetles may not feed at all.

Brown garden snail

Brown garden snails are common in gardens, woods, hedges, and dunes. They have huge appetites, and you can often see nibble marks and holes in the leaves of the plants they munch through.

Garden beetles

Beetles are a common sight in gardens. While some eat living plants, most are helpful bugs because they feed on dead plants and eat other insects that gobble up healthy plants.

A beetle's shiny outer wings look like a shell. They are called elytra. Most beetles can fly, but some have wings that they never use. Other beetles don't have the right kind of wings, so they can't fly.

Brilliant beetles

There are many families of beetles, each with different characteristics. Here are some examples of beetle families.

Ground beetles

Ground beetles are a family of beetles that live mostly in and on soil. They can be black, blue, green, or brown, and are often shiny and metallic.

Soldier beetles

Soldier beetles can be found flying among flowers because they feed on nectar. Beetles in this family can be black or brown with red, yellow, or orange markings.

Rove beetles

Rove beetles are a beetle family that like moist places around decaying plants or animals. They have long bodies, and are black or brown, but some have red markings.

A beetle uses its antennae to touch and smell its surroundings.

Like all insects, beetles have six jointed legs.

Ladybug

This handsome beetle is a ferocious hunter. It eats lots of aphids (greenfly and blackfly), which can damage plants, so it is very helpful to gardeners. Some ladybugs are yellow or orange with black spots.

Around the world, there are about 400,000 species of beetles that we know of. Many more are yet to be discovered.

Follow!

Egg, caterpillar, pupa, butterfly

Some bugs, like butterflies, completely change the way they look as they become adults. A butterfly goes through several changes to become its final form. This amazing life cycle can take a month or even a year.

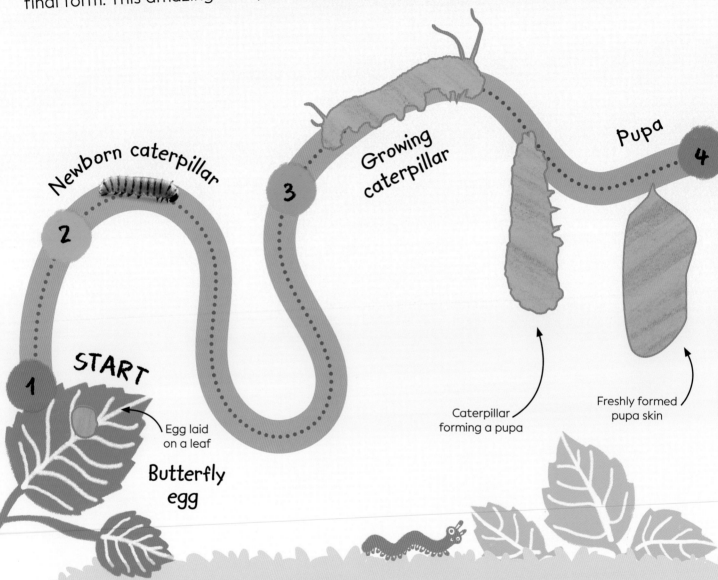

Newborn caterpillar

2

START

1

Egg laid on a leaf

Butterfly egg

3

Growing caterpillar

Pupa

4

Caterpillar forming a pupa

Freshly formed pupa skin

Metamorphosis

Adult butterflies lay eggs. Wriggling caterpillars hatch from the eggs. Each caterpillar that survives, sheds its skin several times and grows bigger. A full-grown caterpillar then forms a pupa. Inside the pupa, the insect changes into a butterfly. Eventually, the butterfly breaks out of the pupa.

This process of an animal changing from one form to another as it grows is called metamorphosis.

Egg

A female butterfly lays her eggs on leaves or on other parts of plants.

Newborn caterpillar

Tiny caterpillars hatch from the eggs. Each caterpillar eats its egg case first, and then goes on to find more food.

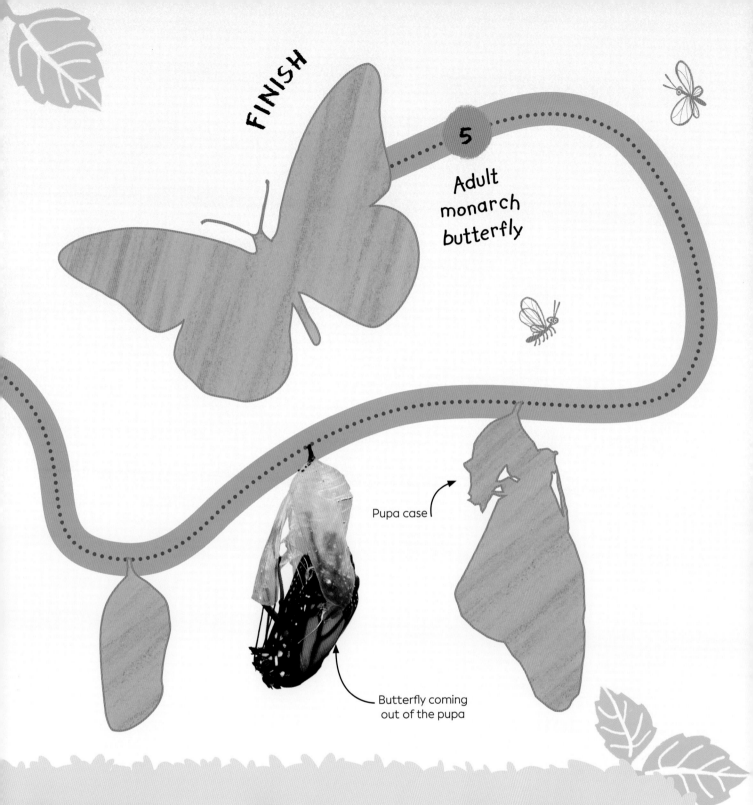

FINISH

5

Adult
monarch
butterfly

Pupa case

Butterfly coming
out of the pupa

 ### Growing caterpillar

The caterpillars continue to eat almost constantly. Each one sheds its skin several times as it grows.

 ### Pupa

A grown caterpillar attaches itself to a stem or twig. It sheds its caterpillar skin and becomes a pupa. A butterfly pupa is also called a chrysalis.

 ### Butterfly

The pupa stage lasts weeks, months, or up to a year, depending on the butterfly species. But eventually, a full-grown butterfly breaks out of its pupa.

Predators

A garden is full of predatory bugs, from hairy spiders to slithery centipedes. Some chase their prey, while others wait to ambush their victims. Bloodsuckers can feed from other animals without killing them, so they are not predators but parasites.

Hornets

The hornet is a kind of large wasp. It eats other insects. Like other wasps, it is a social insect and lives in a nest. Each nest has a queen. She lays eggs that hatch into young hornets called larvae.

Flea

This tiny, biting insect clings to an animal's fur, feathers, or skin. It sucks the animal's blood, then jumps off to find another victim to bite and feed on.

Dragonfly

Expert flyers, dragonflies dart to and fro so fast that they can look like bright flashes in the air. A dragonfly eats other insects, and its huge eyes help it spot prey.

Daddy longlegs

Tiny hooks on this creature's front legs help it snatch worms, snails, and small insects, which it eats. It can't bite, but it defends itself from its enemies by squirting a foul-smelling liquid at them.

Orb-weaver spider

This spider spins a deadly web of silk to trap flying insects. Spider silk is incredibly sticky and stretchy.

Green lacewing

Look out for the lacewing on summer nights. It gets its name from its delicate wings, which have a pattern of veins, and look like fine lace. Lacewing larvae are predators and feed on tiny insects. Adult lacewings feed on nectar and pollen, but some may not feed at all.

Mosquito

Both male and female mosquitoes feed on flower nectar, but only female mosquitoes bite. They need blood to produce eggs, and use their sharp mouthparts to stab the skin of humans and other animals. Then they suck up a little blood.

Granulated ground beetle

During the day, this beetle hides under logs and stones. At night, it comes out to hunt other insects, worms, and slugs. The granulated ground beetle does not fly, but it is a fast runner.

Damselfly

This pretty insect looks like a small, slender dragonfly. It feeds on other insects. Like dragonflies, most damselflies lay their eggs in water, so they are often found near ponds and rivers.

Garden spiders

Fit it!

Spiders are not insects. They are part of another animal group called arachnids. All arachnids have eight legs, whereas all insects have six legs. Like other arachnids, spiders are excellent predators.

There are more than 45,000 species of spiders in the world.

You can't see them, but a spider has sharp mouthparts, which it uses to inject venom into its prey.

Furrow spider

Eight legs

Head and chest (combined together)

Eyes

Two sensory feelers (called palps)

Lower body (called the abdomen)

Follow this picture to make a big spider below!

Spiders eat insects and also other spiders, but they cannot fly to catch them. Some make webs to trap their prey. Others creep up on their victims.

Even though most spiders have eight eyes, many have poor eyesight and rely on their other senses to hunt.

A spider can hear with its legs, which are covered with sensitive hairs that detect sound vibrations.

Spiders use the very tiny hairs on the ends of their legs to help them grip and climb almost any kind of surface.

Furrow spider

Silverfish

This is an insect, not a fish! Silverfish eat many things, including flour, oats, paper, cardboard, clothing, and dead insects. You might find them searching for food in your home.

Mealworms

These wriggly creatures are the larvae of mealworm beetles. They eat dead plants, dead insects, and other dead animals.

Garden ants

Garden ants eat nectar, rotting fruit, and dead insects. Some are also predators, feeding on live insects. Ants leave scent trails to guide other ants in their colony to food sources.

Ants carry food back to their nest. They are so strong that some of them can carry up to 5,000 times their own weight.

Match it!

Scavengers

Most of these bugs do not eat living plants or kill prey—but they eat almost anything else. They consume rotting plants, the dead bodies of other animals, garbage, and our food. One even eats paper and cardboard!

Woodlouse

Woodlice like dark, damp places. They mostly eat rotting wood and other dead plant material.

Bluebottle fly

Bluebottle larvae are scavengers that eat dead animals, dead plants, and poop. Adult bluebottle flies feed on flower nectar.

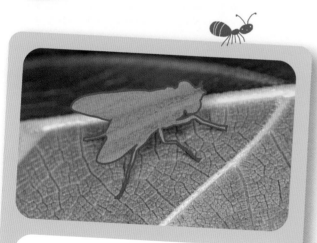

Housefly

Adult houseflies eat a wide variety of food, from fruit to rotting meat. But they can't chew, so they spit on food, then drink the soupy mixture. Housefly larvae eat dead animals, rotting plants, and poop.

Yellow-bellied burying beetle

This beetle belongs to a group of flesh-eating beetles. At night, it flies to find dead animals, which it buries, eats, and also rears its young on. In the daytime, it stays hidden.

1. How many legs do spiders have?

2. Which two creepy-crawlies with similar names have lots of body segments?

3. Name the sweet liquid produced by flowers that butterflies and some other insects drink.

4. Slugs are most active in the daytime. True or false?

6. Like all insects, beetles have six jointed legs. True or false?

5. What word is used for young stag beetles and many other young insects?

Guess it!

Sticker quiz

Reward yourself with a ladybug sticker for each question you answer correctly.

8. Around the world, about how many species of beetles have been discovered so far?

7. When an animal changes from one form to another as it grows, what do we call this process?

10. Where do most dragonflies and damselflies lay their eggs?

9. Ants can carry up to 2,000 times their own weight. True or false?

1. Eight 2. Centipede and millipede 3. Nectar 4. False 5. Larvae 6. True 7. Metamorphosis 8. About 400,000 9. False 10. In water

Find it!

Pages 2-3 Bugs in the garden

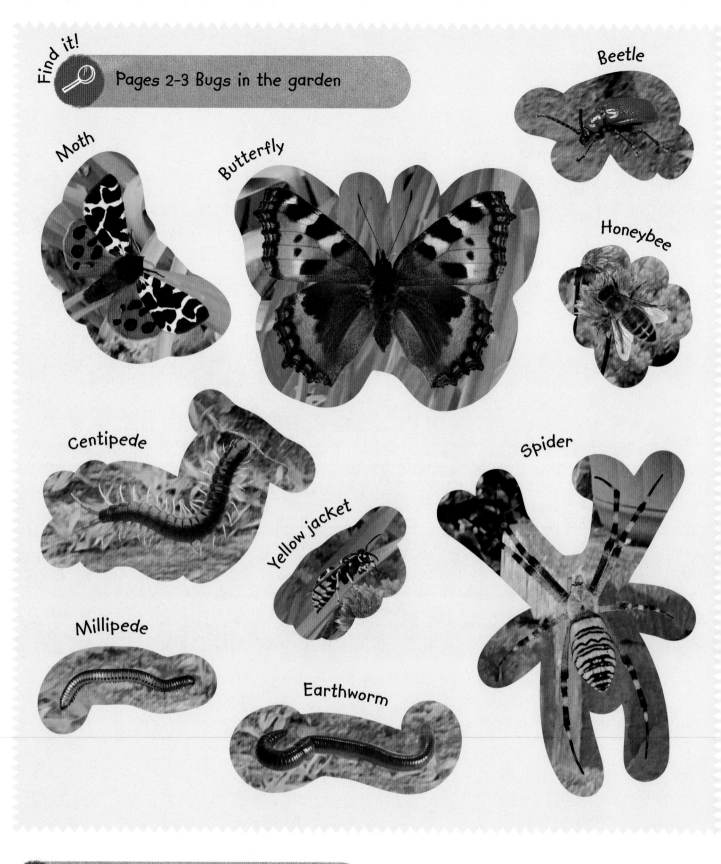

Beetle

Moth

Butterfly

Honeybee

Centipede

Spider

Yellow jacket

Millipede

Earthworm

Extra stickers

Pages 4-5 Plant-eaters

Monarch butterfly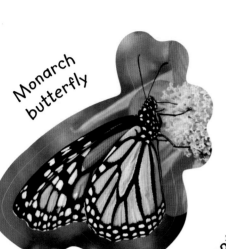

Common garden slug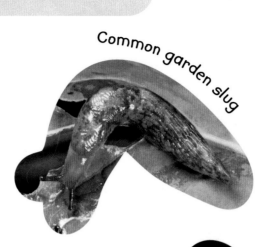

Bumblebee

Puss moth caterpillar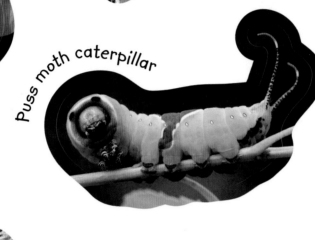

Stag beetle

Hummingbird moth

Brown garden snail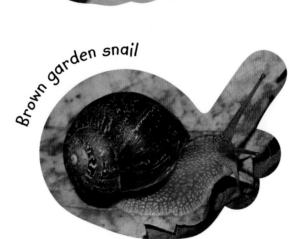

Extra stickers

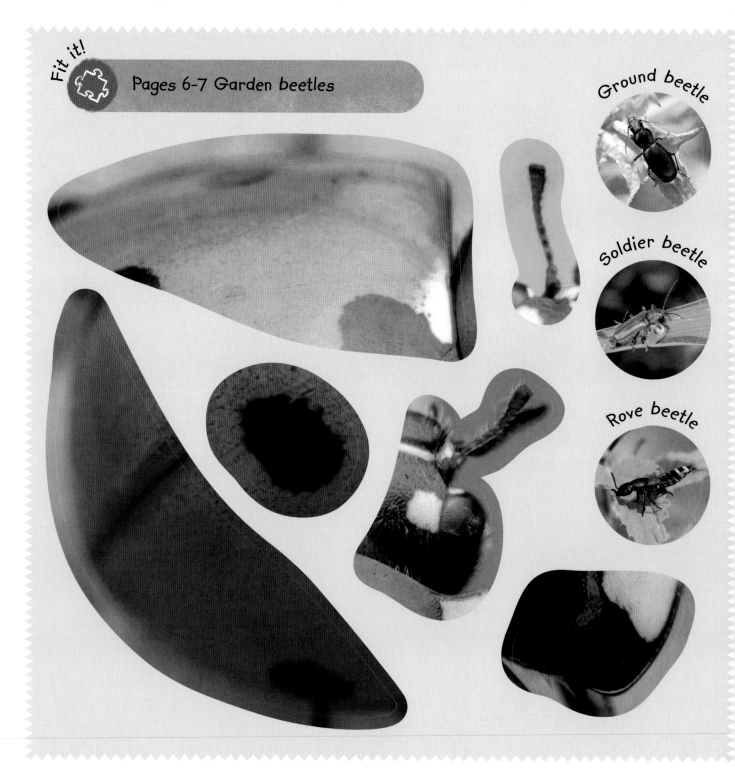

Fit it! Pages 6-7 Garden beetles

Ground beetle

Soldier beetle

Rove beetle

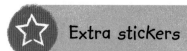

Extra stickers

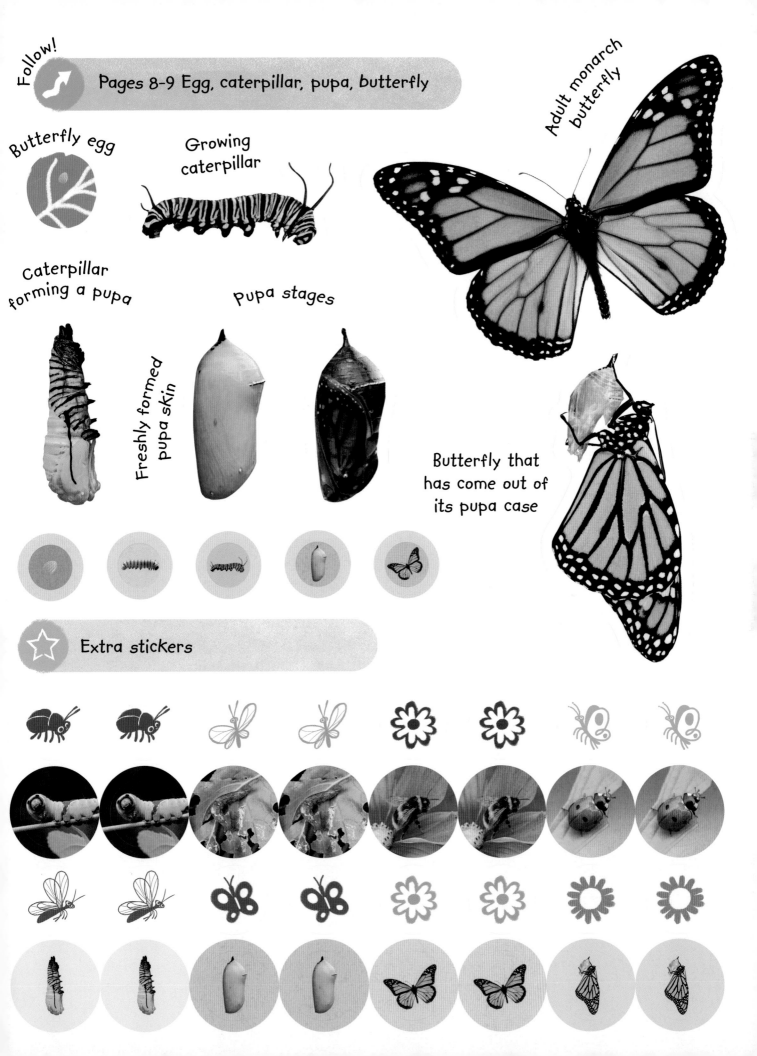

Follow!

Pages 8-9 Egg, caterpillar, pupa, butterfly

Butterfly egg

Growing caterpillar

Adult monarch butterfly

Caterpillar forming a pupa

Pupa stages

Freshly formed pupa skin

Butterfly that has come out of its pupa case

Extra stickers

Mosquito

Flea

Dragonfly's wing

Orb-weaver spider's lower body

Daddy longlegs

Hornet

Green lacewing

Damselfly's wings

Extra stickers

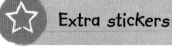

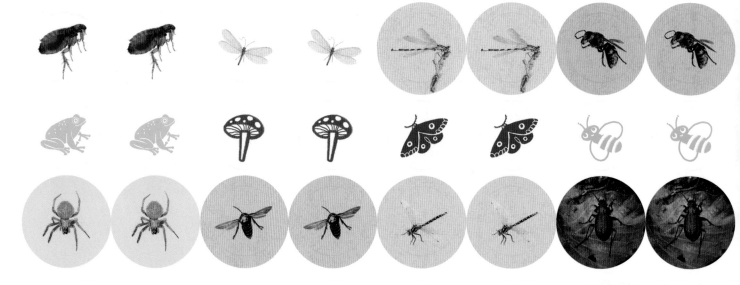

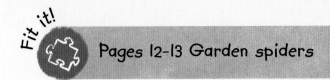

Pages 12-13 Garden spiders

 Extra stickers

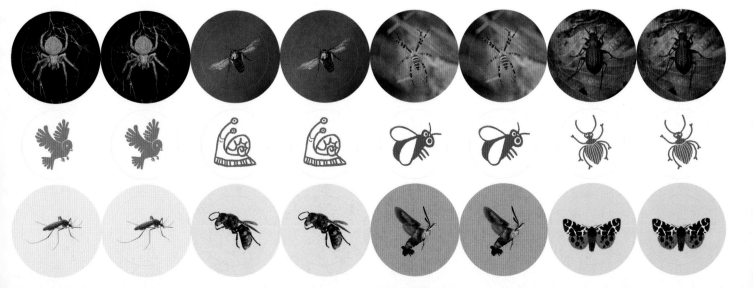

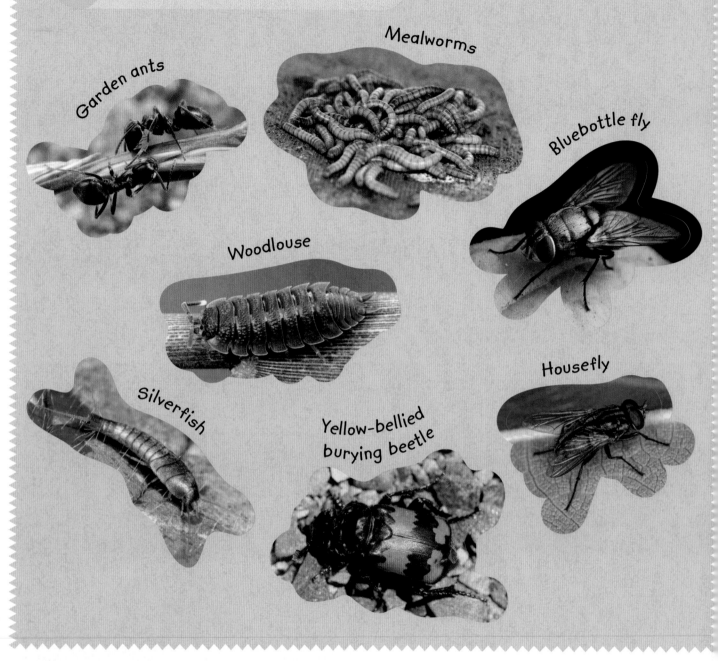

Garden ants

Mealworms

Bluebottle fly

Woodlouse

Silverfish

Yellow-bellied
burying beetle

Housefly

 Extra stickers

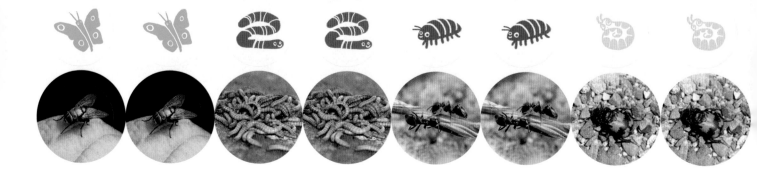

Page 16 Sticker quiz

Extra stickers